The Immutability of God

By Charles Spurgeon

ISBN-13: 978-1986039338

Dear reader,

Thank you for purchasing Charles Spurgeon's classic sermon, *The Immutability of God*. This sermon has blessed millions of believers since its original publication, and The New Christian Classics Library is proud to present it to a new generation of believers.

Care has been taken to preserve the original wording, grammar, and vocabulary of this classic text (including items that would be considered typos or errors by today's publishing standards). By doing so, modern readers will be able to experience and enjoy this sermon as countless believers have before them.

Our prayer is that you will benefit from and be challenged by the message herein, and we commit you and your reading of this book to our great God who always answers our prayers above and beyond anything we could think or imagine.

Sincerely,

The New Christian Classics Library

For more Christian classics, visit our Facebook page at:

www.facebook.com/thenewchristianclassicslibrary

The Immutability of God

• • •

"I am the Lord, I change not; therefore you sons of Jacob are not consumed."

Malachi 3:6

IT has been said by someone that "the proper study of mankind is man." I will not oppose the idea, but I believe it is equally true that the proper study of God's elect is God. The proper study of a Christian is the Godhead. The highest science, the loftiest speculation, the mightiest philosophy which can ever engage the attention of a child of God is the name, the nature, the Person, the work, the doings and the existence of the great God whom he calls his Father. There is something exceedingly improving to the mind in a contemplation of the Divinity. It is a subject so vast, that all our thoughts are lost in its immensity—so deep that our pride is drowned in its infinity.

Other subjects we can compass and grapple with—in them we feel a kind of self-content and go our way with the thought, "Behold I am wise." But when we come to this master science, finding that our plumb line cannot sound its depth and that our eagle eye cannot see its height, we turn away with the thoughts that vain man would be wise, but he is like a wild ass's colt and with the solemn exclamation, "I am but of yesterday and know nothing." No subject of contemplation will tend more to humble the mind, than thoughts of God. We shall be obliged to feel—

"Great God, how infinite are You,
What worthless worms are we!"

But while the subject humbles the mind it also expands it. He who often thinks of God will have a larger mind than the man who simply plods around this narrow globe. He may be a naturalist, boasting of his ability to dissect a beetle, anatomize a fly, or arrange insects and animals in classes with well-nigh unutterable names. He may be a geologist, able to discourse of the megatherium and the plesiosaurus and all kinds of extinct animals. He may imagine that his science, whatever it is, ennobles and enlarges his mind. I dare say it does, but after all, the most excellent study for expanding the soul is the science of Christ and Him crucified and the knowledge of the Godhead in the glorious Trinity.

Nothing will so enlarge the intellect, nothing so magnify the whole soul of man as a devout, earnest, continued investigation of the great subject of the Deity. And while humbling and expanding, this subject is eminently consolatory. Oh, there is, in contemplating Christ, a balm for every wound! In musing on the Father, there is a quietus for every grief and in the influence of the Holy Spirit there is a balsam for every sore. Would you lose your sorrows? Would you drown your cares? Then go plunge yourself in the Godhead's deepest sea–be lost in His immensity. And you shall come forth as from a couch of rest, refreshed and invigorated.

I know nothing which can so comfort the soul, so calm the swelling billows of grief and sorrow–so speak peace to the winds of trial–as a devout musing upon the subject of the Godhead. It is to that subject that I invite you this morning. We shall present you with one view of it–that is the immutability of the glorious Jehovah. "I am," says my text, "Jehovah," (for so it should be translated) "I am Jehovah, I change not; therefore you sons of Jacob are not consumed."

There are three things this morning. First of all, an unchanging God. Secondly, the persons who derive benefit from this glorious attribute, "the sons of Jacob." And thirdly, the benefit they so derive, they "are not consumed." We address ourselves to these points.

First of all, we have set before us the doctrine of THE IMMUTABILITY OF GOD. "I am God, I change not." Here I shall attempt to expound, or rather to enlarge the thought and then afterwards to bring a few arguments to prove its truth.

I shall offer some exposition of my text by first saying that God is Jehovah and He changes not in His essence. We cannot tell you what Godhead is. We do not know what substance that is which we call God. It is an existence, it is a Being. But what that is we know not. However, whatever it is, we call it His essence and that essence never changes. The substance of mortal things is ever changing. The mountains with their snow-white crowns doff their old diadems in summer, in rivers trickling down their sides, while the storm cloud gives them another coronation. The ocean, with its mighty floods, loses its water when the sunbeams kiss the waves and snatch them in mists to Heaven. Even the sun himself requires fresh fuel from the hand of the Infinite Almighty to replenish his ever-burning furnace.

All creatures change. Man, especially as to his body, is always undergoing revolution. Very probably there is not a single particle in my body which was in it a few years ago. This frame has been worn away by activity, its atoms have been removed by friction, fresh particles of matter have in the meantime constantly accrued to my body and so it has been replenished—its substance is altered. The fabric of which this world is made is ever passing away like a stream of water—drops are running away and others are following after, keeping the river still full—but always changing in its elements.

But God is perpetually the same. He is not composed of any substance or material, but is spirit-pure, essential and ethereal spirit—and therefore He is immutable. He remains everlastingly the same. There are no furrows on His eternal brow. No age has palsied Him—no years have marked Him with the mementoes of their flight. He sees ages pass, but with Him it is ever now. He is the great I AM—the Great Unchangeable. Mark you, His essence did not undergo a change when it became united with the manhood. When Christ in past years did gird Himself with mortal clay, the essence of His divinity was not changed—flesh did not become God, nor did God become flesh by a real actual change of nature.

The two were united in hypostatical union, but the Godhead was still the same. It was the same when He was a babe in the manger, as it was when He stretched the curtains of Heaven—it was the same God that hung upon the Cross and whose blood flowed down in a purple river. The self-same God that holds the world upon His everlasting shoulders and bears in His hands the keys of death and Hell. He never has been changed in His essence, not even by His incarnation– He remains everlastingly, eternally, the one unchanging God, the Father of lights, with whom there is no variableness, neither the shadow of a change.

He changes not in His attributes. Whatever the attributes of God were of old, they are the same now. And of each of them we may sing, As it was in the beginning, is now and ever shall be, world without end, Amen. Was He powerful? Was He the mighty God when He spoke the world out of the womb of non-existence? Was He the Omnipotent when He piled the mountains and scooped out the hollow places for the rolling deep? Yes, He was powerful then and His arm is unpalsied now. He is the same giant in His might. The sap of His nourishment is still wet and the strength of His soul stands the same forever.

Was He wise when He constituted this mighty globe, when He laid the foundations of the universe? Had He wisdom when He planned the way of our salvation and when from all eternity He marked out His awful plans? Yes and He is wise now. He is not less skillful, He has not less knowledge. His eyes which sees all things are undimmed. His ears which hear all the cries, sighs, sobs and groans of His people, are not rendered heavy by the years which He has heard their prayers. He is unchanged in His wisdom. He knows as much now as ever–neither more nor less.

He has the same consummate skill and the same infinite forecasting. He is unchanged, blessed be His name, in His justice. Just and holy was He in the past–just and holy is He now. He is unchanged in His Truth–He has promised and He brings it to pass. He has said it and it shall be done. He varies not in the goodness, generosity and benevolence of His nature. He is not become an Almighty tyrant, whereas He was once an Almighty Father. His strong love stands like a granite rock unmoved by the hurricanes of our iniquity. And blessed be His dear name, He is unchanged in His love. When He first wrote the Covenant, how full His heart was with affection to His people. He knew that His Son must die to ratify the articles of that agreement. He knew right well that He must rend His best Beloved from His heart and send Him down to earth to bleed and die.

He did not hesitate to sign that mighty covenant. Nor did He shun its fulfillment. He loves as much now as He did then. And when suns shall cease to shine and moons to show their feeble light, He still shall love on forever and forever. Take any one attribute of God and I will write semper idem on it (always the same). Take any one thing you can say of God now and it may be said not only in the dark past, but in the bright future. It shall always remain the same–"I am Jehovah, I change not"–impressed on His heart it remains.

Then again, God changes not in His plans. That man began to build, but was not able to finish and therefore he changed his plan–as every wise man would do in such a case–he built upon a smaller foundation and commenced again. But has it ever been said that God began to build but was not able to finish? No. When He has boundless stores at His command and when His own right hand would create worlds as numerous as drops of morning dew, shall He ever stay because He has not power? Or reverse, or alter, or disarrange His plan because He cannot carry it out?

"But," say some, "perhaps God never had a plan." Do you think God is more foolish than yourself then, Sir? Do you go to work without a plan? "No," you say, "I have always a scheme." So has God. Every man has his plan and God has a plan, too. God is a master-mind–He arranged everything in His gigantic intellect long before He did it–and once having settled it, mark you, He never alters it. "This shall be done," says He and the iron hand of destiny marks it down and it is brought to pass. "This is My purpose," and it stands, nor can earth or Hell alter it. "This is My decree," says

He. Promulgate it angels–rend it down from the gate of Heaven you devils. But you cannot alter the decree. It shall be done.

God alters not His plans–why should He? He is Almighty and therefore can perform His pleasure. Why should He? He is the All-wise and therefore cannot have planned wrongly. Why should He? He is the everlasting God and therefore cannot die before His plan is accomplished. Why should He change? You worthless atoms of existence, ephemera of the day! You creeping insects upon this bay-leaf of existence! You may change your plans, but He shall never, never change His. Then has He told me that His plan is to save me? If so, I am safe–

> *"My name from the palms of His hands*
> *Eternity will not erase;*
> *Impressed on His heart it remains,*
> *In marks of indelible grace."*

Yet again, God is unchanging in His promises. Ah, we love to speak about the sweet promises of God. But if we could ever suppose that one of them could be changed–we would not talk anything more about them. If I thought that the notes of the bank of England could not be cashed next week, I should decline to take them and if I thought that God's promises would never be fulfilled–if I thought that

God would see it right to alter some word in His promises—farewell Scriptures! I want immutable things—and I find that I have immutable promises when I turn to the Bible—for, "by two immutable things in which it is impossible for God to lie," He has signed, confirmed and sealed every promise of His.

The Gospel is not "yes and no," it is not promising today and denying tomorrow. The Gospel is "yes, yes," to the glory of God. Believer! There was a delightful promise which you had yesterday—and this morning when you turned to the Bible the promise was not sweet. Do you know why? Do you think the promise had changed? Ah, no, you changed—that is where the matter lies. You had been eating some of the grapes of Sodom and your mouth was thereby put out of taste and you could not detect the sweetness. But there was the same honey there, depend upon it— the same preciousness. "Oh," says one child of God, "I had built my house firmly once upon some stable promises. There came a wind and I said, O Lord, I am cast down and I shall be lost."

Oh, the promises were not cast down. The foundations were not removed. It was your little "wood, hay, stubble" hut that you had been building. It was that which fell down. You have been shaken on the rock, not the rock under you. But let me tell you what is the best way of living in the world. I have heard that a gentleman said to a Negro, "I can't think how it is you are always so happy in the Lord and I am often downcast." "Why Massa," said he, "I throw myself flat down on the promise–there I lie. You stand on the promise–you have a little to do with it and down you go when the wind comes. And then you cry, 'Oh, I am down.' Whereas I go flat on the promise at once and that is why I fear no fall."

Then let us always say, "Lord there is the promise. It is your business to fulfill it." Down I go on the promise flat! No standing up for me. That is where you should go–prostrate on the promise. And remember, every promise is a rock, an unchanging thing. Therefore, at His feet cast yourself and rest there forever.

But now comes one jarring note to spoil the theme. To some of you God is unchanging in His threats. If every promise stands fast and every oath of the Covenant is fulfilled, hark you, Sinner–mark the word–hear the death-knell of your carnal hopes! See the funeral of the fleshy trusting. Every threat of God, as well as every promise shall be fulfilled. Talk of decrees! I will tell you of a decree –"He that believes not shall be damned." That is a decree and a statute that can never change. Be as good as you please, be as moral as you can, be as honest as you will, walk as uprightly as you may—there stands the unchangeable threat - "He that believes not shall be damned."

What do you say to that, Moralist? Oh, you wish you could alter it and say, "He that does not live a holy life shall be damned." That will be true. But it does not say so. It says, "He that believes not." Here is the stone of stumbling and the rock of offense. But you cannot alter it—you either believe or be damned, says the Bible. And mark—that threat of God is as unchangeable as God Himself. And when a thousand years of Hell's torments shall have passed away you shall look on high and see written in burning letters of fire, "He that believes not shall be damned."

"But, Lord, I am damned." Nevertheless it says "shall be" still. And when a million years have rolled away and you are exhausted by your pains and agonies you shall turn up your eye and still read "SHALL BE DAMNED," unchanged, unaltered. And when you shall have thought that eternity must have spun out its last thread—that every particle of that which we call eternity must have run out, you shall still see it written up there, "SHALL BE DAMNED." O terrible thought! How dare I utter it? But I must. You must be warned, Sirs, "lest you also come into this place of torment." You must be told rough things for if God's Gospel is not a rough thing, believe me, the Law is a rough thing.

Mount Sinai is a rough thing. Woe unto the watchman that warns not the ungodly! God is unchanging in His threats. Beware, O Sinner, for "it is a fearful thing to fall into the hands of the living God."

We must just hint at one thought before we pass on and that is–God is unchanging in the objects of His love–not only in His love, but in the objects of it–

> *"If ever it should come to pass*
> *That sheep of Christ might fall away,*
> *My fickle, feeble soul, alas,*
> *Would fall a thousand times a day."*

If one dear saint of God had perished, so might all. If one of the Covenant Ones is lost, so may all be and then there is no Gospel promise true. Then the Bible is a lie and there is nothing in it worth my acceptance. I will be an infidel at once, when I can believe that a saint of God can ever fall finally. If God has loved me once, then He will love me forever–

> *"Did Jesus once upon me shine,*
> *Then Jesus is forever mine"*

The objects of everlasting love never change. Those whom God has called, He will justify. Whom He has justified, He will sanctify. And whom He sanctifies, He will glorify.

Thus having taken a great deal too much time, perhaps, in simply expanding the thought of an unchanging God, I will now try to prove that He is unchangeable. I am not much of an argumentative preacher, but one argument that I will mention is this–the very existence and Being of a God seem to me to imply immutability. Let me think a moment. There is a God. This God rules and governs all things–this God fashioned the world–He upholds and maintains it. What kind of Being must He be? It does strike me that you cannot think of a changeable God. I conceive that the thought is so repugnant to common sense that if you for one moment think of a changing God, the words seem to clash and you are obliged to say, "Then He must be a kind of man," and you have a Mormonism idea of God.

I imagine it is impossible to conceive of a changing God. It is so to me. Others may be capable of such an idea, but I could not entertain it. I could no more think of a changing God than I could of a round square, or any other absurdity. The thing seems so contrary that I am obliged, when once I say God, to include the idea of an unchanging Being.

Well, I think that one argument will be enough, but another good argument may be found in the fact of God's perfection. I believe God to be a perfect Being. Now, if He is a perfect Being, He cannot change. Do you not see this? Suppose I am perfect today. If it were possible for me to change, should I be perfect tomorrow after the alteration? If I changed, I must either change from a good state to a better–and then if I could get better, I could not be perfect now–or else from a better state to a worse–and if I were worse, I should not be perfect then. If I am perfect, I cannot be altered without being imperfect. If I am perfect today, I must be the same tomorrow if I am to be perfect then. So, if God is perfect, He must be the same–for change would imply imperfection now, or imperfection then.

Again, there is the fact of God's infinity, which puts change out of the question. God is an infinite Being. What do you mean by that? There is no man who can tell you what he means by an infinite being. But there cannot be two infinities. If one thing is infinite, there is no room for anything else–for infinite means all. It means not bounded, not finite, having no end. Well, there cannot be two infinities. If God is infinite today and then should change and be infinite tomorrow there would be two infinities. But that cannot be.

Suppose He is infinite and then changes, He must become finite and could not be God–either He is finite today and finite tomorrow, or infinite today and finite tomorrow, or finite today and infinite tomorrow–all of which suppositions are equally absurd. The fact of His being an infinite Being at once quashes the thought of His being a changeable Being. Infinity has written on its very brow the word "immutability."

But then, dear Friends, let us look at the past–and there we shall gather some proofs of God's immutable nature. "Has He spoken and has He not done it? Has He sworn and has it not come to pass?" Can it not be said of Jehovah, He has done all His will and He has accomplished all His purpose? "Turn you to Philistia–ask where she is. God said, "Howl Ashdod and you gates of Gaza, for you shall fall," and where are they? Where is Edom? Ask Petra and its ruined walls. Will they not echo back the truth that God has said, "Edom shall be a prey and shall be destroyed"? Where is Babel and where is Nineveh? Where is Moab and where is Ammon? Where are the nations God has said He would destroy? Has He not uprooted them and cast out the remembrance of them from the earth?

And has God cast off His people? Has He once been unmindful of His promise? Has He once broken His oath and covenant, or once departed from His plan? Ah, no. Point to one instance in history where God has changed! You cannot Sirs–for throughout all history there stands the fact–God has been immutable in His purposes. Methinks I hear someone say, "I can remember one passage in Scripture where God changed!" And so did I think once. The case I mean, is that of the death of Hezekiah. Isaiah came in and said, "Hezekiah, you must die, your disease is incurable, set your house in order."

He turned his face to the wall and began to pray. And before Isaiah was in the outer court, he was told to go back and say, "you shall live fifteen years more." You may think that proves that God changes. But really, I cannot see in it the slightest proof in the world. How do you know that God did not know that? Oh, but God did know it–He knew that Hezekiah would live. Then He did not change, for if He knew that, how could He change? That is what I want to know. But do you know one little thing? - that Hezekiah's son Manasseh was not born at that time. And had Hezekiah died there would have been no Manasseh and no Josiah and no Christ, because Christ came from that very line!

You will find that Manasseh was twelve years old when His father died–so that He must have been born three years after this. And do you not believe that God decreed the birth of Manasseh and foreknew it? Certainly. Then He decreed that Isaiah should go and tell Hezekiah that his disease was incurable and then say also in the same breath, "But I will cure it and you shall live." He said that to stir up Hezekiah to prayer.

He spoke, in the first place as a man. "According to all human probability your disease is incurable and you must die." Then He waited till Hezekiah prayed–then came a little "but" at the end of the sentence.

Isaiah had not finished the sentence. He said, "you must put your house in order for there is no human cure–but" (and then he walked out. Hezekiah prayed a little and then he came in again and said) "But I will heal you." Where is there any contradiction there, except in the brain of those who fight against the Lord and wish to make Him a changeable being?

Now secondly, let me say a word on THE PERSONS TO WHOM THIS UNCHANGEABLE GOD IS A BENEFIT. "I am God I change not; therefore you sons of Jacob are not consumed." Now, who are "the sons of Jacob"? Who can rejoice in an immutable God?

First, they are the sons of God's election. For it is written, "Jacob have I loved and Esau have I hated, the children being not yet born, neither having done good nor evil." It was written, "The elder shall serve the younger." "The sons of Jacob -

"Are the sons of God's election,
Who through sovereign grace believe;
By eternal destination
Grace and glory they receive."

God's elect are here meant by "the sons of Jacob"–
those whom He foreknew and foreordained to
everlasting salvation.

By "the sons of Jacob" are meant, in the second place,
persons who enjoy peculiar rights and titles. Jacob,
you know, had no rights by birth, but he soon
acquired them. He exchanged a mess of pottage with
his brother Esau and thus gained the birthright. I do
not justify the means. But he did also obtain the
blessing and so acquired peculiar rights. By "the sons
of Jacob" is meant persons who have peculiar rights
and titles. Unto them that believe, He has given the
right the gates into the city"–they have a title to eternal
honors. They have a promise to everlasting glory.
They have a right to call themselves sons of God. Oh,
there are peculiar rights and privileges belonging to
the "sons of Jacob."

Next, these "sons of Jacob" were men of peculiar
manifestations. Jacob had had peculiar manifestations
from his God and thus he was highly honored. Once
at night he lay down and slept. He had the hedges for
his curtains, the sky for his canopy, a stone for his

pillow and the earth for his bed. Oh, then he had a peculiar manifestation. There was a ladder and he saw the angels of God ascending and descending. He thus had a manifestation of Christ Jesus as the ladder which reaches from earth to Heaven–up and down which angels came to bring us mercies.

Then what a manifestation there was at Mahanaim when the angels of God met him–and again at Peniel, when He wrestled with God and saw Him face to face. Those were peculiar manifestations–and this passage refers to those who, like Jacob, have had peculiar manifestations.

Now then, how many of you have had personal manifestations? "Oh," you say "that is enthusiasm– that is fanaticism." Well it is a blessed enthusiasm, too, for the sons of Jacob have had peculiar manifestations. They have talked with God as a man talks with his friend–they have whispered in the ear of Jehovah. Christ has been with them to sup with them and they with Christ. And the Holy Spirit has shone into their souls with such a mighty radiance that they could not doubt about special manifestations. The "sons of Jacob" are the men who enjoy these manifestations.

Then again, they are men of peculiar trials. Ah, poor Jacob! I should not choose Jacob's lot if I had not the prospect of Jacob's blessing. For a hard lot his was. He had to run away from his father's house to Laban's–and then that surly old Laban cheated him all the years he was there–cheated him of his wife, cheated him in his wages, cheated him in his flocks and cheated him all through the story. By-and-by he had to run away from Laban who pursued him and overtook him.

Next came Esau with four hundred men to cut him up root and branch. Then there was a season of prayer and afterwards he wrestled God–and had to go all his life with his thigh out of joint. But a little further on, Raphael, his dearly beloved, died. Then his daughter Dinah is led astray and the sons murder the Shechemites. Then his dear son, Joseph, is sold into Egypt and a famine comes. Then Reuben goes up to his couch and pollutes it–Judah commits incest with his own daughter-in-law and all his sons become a plague to him.

At last Benjamin is taken away and the old man, almost broken-hearted, Cries, "Joseph is not and Simeon is not and you will take Benjamin away?" Never was man more tried than Jacob–all through the one sin of cheating his brother. All through his life God chastised him. But I believe there are many who can sympathize with dear old Jacob. They have had to pass through trials very much like his. Well, crossbearers, God says, "I change not; therefore you sons of Jacob are not consumed." Poor tried Souls! You are not consumed because of the unchanging nature of your God.

Now do not get to fretting and say, with the self-conceit of misery, "I am the man who has seen affliction." Why "the Man of Sorrows" was afflicted more than you! Jesus was indeed a mourner. You only see the skirts of the garments of affliction. You never have trials like His. You do not understand what troubles mean. You have hardly sipped the cup of trouble–you have only had a drop or two, but Jesus drunk the dregs. Fear not, says God, "I am the Lord, I change not; therefore you sons of Jacob," men of peculiar trials, "are not consumed."

Then one more thought about who are the "sons of Jacob," for I should like you to find out whether you are "sons of Jacob," yourselves. They are men of peculiar character. For though there were some things about Jacob's character which we cannot commend, there are one or two things which God commends. There was Jacob's faith, by which Jacob had his name written among the mighty worthies who obtained not the promises on earth but shall obtain them in Heaven. Are you men of faith, Beloved? Do you know what it is to walk by faith, to live by faith, to get your temporary food by faith, to live on spiritual manna–all by faith? Is faith the rule of your life? If so, you are the "sons of Jacob."

Then Jacob was a man of prayer–a man who wrestled and groaned and prayed. There is a man up yonder who never prayed this morning, before coming up to the house of God. Ah, you poor Heathen, don't you pray? "No!" he says, "I never thought of such a thing–for years I have not prayed." Well, I hope you may before you die. Live and die without prayer and you will pray long enough when you get to Hell. There is a woman–she did not pray this morning. She was so busy sending her children to the Sunday-School she had no time to pray. No time to pray? Had you time to dress? There is a time for every purpose under Heaven and if you had purposed to pray, you would have prayed.

Sons of God cannot live without prayer. They are wrestling Jacobs. They are men in whom the Holy Spirit so works that they can no more live without prayer than I can live without breathing. They must pray. Sirs, mark you, if you are living without prayer, you are living without Christ. And dying like that, your portion will be in the lake which burns with fire. God redeem you, God rescue you from such a lot! But you who are "the sons of Jacob," take comfort, for God is immutable.

Thirdly, I can say only a word about the other point–
THE BENEFIT WHICH THESE "SONS OF
JACOB" RECEIVE FROM AN UNCHANGING
GOD.

"Therefore you sons Jacob are not consumed."
"Consumed?" How? How can man be consumed?
Why, there are two ways. We might have been
consumed in Hell. If God had been a changing God,
the "sons of Jacob" here this morning, might have
been consumed in Hell. But for God's unchanging
love I should have been a stick in the fire. But there is
a way of being consumed in this world. There is such
a thing as being condemned before you die–
"condemned already." There is such a thing as being
alive and yet being absolutely dead. We might have
been left to our own devices–and then where should
we have been now?

Reveling with the drunkard, blaspheming Almighty
God? Oh, had He left you, dearly Beloved, had He
been a changing God–you had been among the
filthiest of the filthy and the vilest of the vile. Cannot
you remember in your life seasons similar to those I
have felt? I have gone right to the edge of sin–some
strong temptation has taken hold of both my arms so
that I could not wrestle with it. I have been pushed
along, dragged as by an awful Satanic power to the
very edge of some horrid precipice. I have looked

down, down, down and seen my portion. I quivered on the brink of ruin. I have been horrified, as, with my hair upright, I have thought of the sin I was about to commit—the horrible pit into which I was about to fall.

A strong arm has saved me. I have started back and cried, O God, could I have gone so near sin and yet come back again? Could I have walked right up to the furnace and not fallen down, like Nebuchadnezzar's strong men, devoured by the very heat? Oh, is it possible I should be here this morning, when I think of the sins I have committed and the crimes which have crossed my wicked imagination? Yes, I am here, unconsumed, because the Lord changes not. Oh, if He had changed, we should have been consumed in a dozen ways. If the Lord had changed, you and I should have been consumed by ourselves—for after all, Mr. Self is the worst enemy a Christian has.

We should have proved suicides to our own souls. We should have mixed the cup of poison for our own spirits, if the Lord had not been an unchanging God and dashed the cup out of our hands when we were about to drink it. Then we should have been consumed by God Himself if He had not been a changeless God. We call God a Father—but there is not a father in this world who would not have killed all his children long ago, so provoked would he have been with them–if he had been half as much troubled as God has been with His family. He has the most troublesome family in the whole world–unbelieving, ungrateful, disobedient, forgetful, rebellious, wandering, murmuring and stiff-necked. Well it is that He is long-suffering, or else He would have taken not only the rod, but the sword to some of us long ago.

But there was nothing in us to love at first, so there cannot be less now. John Newton used to tell a whimsical story and laugh at it, too, of a good woman who said, in order to prove the doctrine of Election– "Ah, Sir, the Lord must have loved me before I was born, or else He would not have seen anything in me to love afterwards." I am sure it is true in my case and true in respect to most of God's people. For there is little to love in them after they are born. If He had not loved them before then He would have seen no reason to choose them after–but since He loved them without works, He loves them without works still. Since their good works did not win His affection, bad works cannot sever that affection–since their righteousness did not bind His love to them, so their wickedness cannot snap the golden links.

He loved them out of pure sovereign grace and He will love them still. But we should have been consumed by the devil and by our enemies–consumed by the world, consumed by our sins, by our trials and in a hundred other ways if God had ever changed.

Well, now, time fails us and I can say but little. I have only just cursorily touched on the text. I now hand it to you. May the Lord help you "sons of Jacob" to take home this portion of meat. Digest it well and feed upon it. May the Holy Spirit sweetly apply the glorious things that are written! And may you have "a feast of fat things, of wines on the lees well refined!" Remember God is the same, whatever is removed. Your friends may be disaffected, your ministers may be taken away, everything may change—but God does not. Your Brethren may chance and cast out your name as vile—but God will love you still.

Let your station in life change and your property be gone. Let your whole life be shaken and you become weak and sickly. Let everything flee away—there is one place where change cannot put his finger. There is one name on which mutability can never be written. There is one heart which never can alter. That heart is God's—that name Love -

"Trust Him, He will never deceive you.
Though you hardly of Him deem;
He will never, never leave you,
Nor will let you quite leave Him."

Printed in Great Britain
by Amazon

37131347R00020